99
WAYS TO GET
KIDS TO
LOVE WRITING

Also by
MARY LEONHARDT

*Parents Who Love Reading,
Kids Who Don't*

Keeping Kids Reading

*99 Ways to Get Kids to
Love Reading*

99

Ways To Get Kids to Love Writing

AND **10** EASY TIPS FOR TEACHING THEM GRAMMAR

MARY LEONHARDT

THREE RIVERS PRESS
NEW YORK

Published by Three Rivers Press, a division of Crown Publishers, Inc.,
201 East 50th Street, New York, New York 10022. Member of the
Crown Publishing Group.

Random House, Inc. New York, Toronto, London, Sydney, Auckland

www.randomhouse.com

THREE RIVERS PRESS and colophon are trademarks of
Crown Publishers, Inc.

Printed in the United States of America

Design by Kay Em

Library of Congress Cataloging-in-Publication Data
Leonhardt, Mary.
    99 ways to get kids to love writing, and ten easy tips for
teaching them grammar / Mary Leonhardt. — 1st ed.
        p.   cm.
    1. English language—Composition and exercises—Study and
teaching.   2. English language—Grammar—Study and teaching.
I. Title.
LB1576.L483   1998
808'.042'07—dc21   98-21340
                                              CIP

ISBN 0-609-80320-4

10 9 8 7 6 5 4 3 2 1

CONTENTS

Special Thanks to:

Rich Tombeno, Rachel Ropeik, and Alyssa Galeros for letting me use their writing.

All of my students over the years, who have taught me most of what I know about writing.

My husband, Richard, and my children, Julie, Tim, and Molly, for their love and encouragement.

Introduction

I've known for years how to turn children into wonderful readers. The trick is to help them, as soon as you can, develop a passion for any kind of reading at all. I've written extensively about how to do this in my earlier books.

But it took me years to make the writing connection. While I always tried to have my students do some fun, creative writing activities, I mostly went along teaching writing the same old boring way. "Write an essay about the imagery in this novel," I might say. Or "Here's how to do a character description."

Every so often I'd have a few students who wrote simply dazzling character or theme essays, essays that had a richness and personality completely lacking in the work of their classmates. How did they learn to write like that?

Well, they told me. Just as kids who can read and understand difficult, complex literature have a background of reading anything they can get their hands on, the best writers have a background of doing plenty of writing just for the fun of it. They wrote songs and poetry. They left a trail of locked diaries scattered throughout their childhood. They entertained themselves in boring history classes by writing stories in their history notebooks. One girl told me she wrote her best poetry during physics lectures. They wrote anywhere and everywhere, and by the time they were writing in my English classroom, they were light-years ahead of their classmates.

What follows in this book is much of what they told me about how they developed their love of writing. Based on the new realizations that I've come to, I teach writing completely differently now. Along with the traditional forms (literary essays, research papers, etc.), my students do a great deal of independent, creative writing—and I am getting, by far, the best writing I've ever seen in twenty-eight years of teaching English.

Once kids fall in love with writing, their writing just takes off. It's really worth it, as a parent, to spend a bit of time understanding how to make this happen. So read on! And I'd love to hear comments or suggestions. You can write to me c/o Crown Publishing, 201 E. 50th Street, New York, NY 10022, or E-mail me at maryl@tiac.net.

PART I:
WHY LOVING WRITING
IS IMPORTANT

1

A passion for an activity is the prerequisite for success in any field. Writing is no different.

We have a cultural belief, probably inherited from our Puritan ancestors, that learning should be "rigorous" and a bit unpleasant. To see rows of children glumly attempting to write tightly structured analytical essays—while dreaming of being out on a baseball field—gives us that wonderful, satisfied, sanctimonious, adult feeling that we're training our children well.

But we're not. Just as a baseball team composed of players who hate and dread the game has little chance of winning, children who hate and dread writing have little chance of writing well.

2

Only children who love writing write with the frequency and care necessary for them to become excellent writers.

The average junior-high or high-school English teacher has a hundred and fifty students, and forty-five minutes of preparation time a day. The average elementary-school teacher has twenty-five children, and little, if any, preparation time every day—and she's teaching six or seven completely different subjects.

This means that most students are asked to do very little writing in school. It takes at least ten or fifteen minutes to respond thoughtfully to a piece of writing, and few teachers have that kind of time. A week's writing for one hundred and fifty students would take a teacher about thirty hours of grading time.

The result is that only students who have an independent writing life outside of school learn to write really well—because they are the only students who really get any practice.

What if we tried to develop outstanding tennis players by having them on the court only an hour or two once every three or four weeks? That's a joke, right? Yet that's what happens in schools with writing.

3

Only students who love writing, and write extensively on their own, develop their own voice and personal style.

We are inundated with dreary, voiceless, muddy prose today. Open any textbook. Read most business writing. Read education writing. Writers who are really readable are those who write with some personality—with a little humor, or some embedded imagery, or an authoritative, distinctive tone. Writers who only do academic or business writing have an extraordinarily hard time developing a distinctive style.

I once asked my daughter, a college soccer coach who has done extensive recruiting for a number of Division I universities, what a top player looks like. "They're called 'personality prayers,'" Julie told me. "When they get on a field they make things happen."

Really top writers are "personality writers," and by doing only school writing, it's almost impossible to acquire that sense of language, that fresh outlook and individual voice, that characterizes their work.

4. **Only kids with an independent writing life learn how to write with a sharp, clear focus.**

Since most testing is objective, students don't learn how to compose or focus their thoughts themselves, an essential requirement for the workplace. After all, when you walk into your boss's office with a proposal for a new program, he doesn't say, "Okay, is your program (A) risky but perhaps have the potential to increase profits? (B) safe but in need of a large capital investment? or (C) somewhat safe, if sales..." Well, you get the idea. The boss will say, "Tell me about the program. Why should we use it?" Children who have spent thousands of hours focusing their ideas in various pieces of writing are going to be much better prepared, as adults, to present their ideas with clarity and force.

I also think there is a cautious, dreary element to much academic writing, perhaps because it is written to impress a teacher, or an editor of an arcane academic journal. Vivid, readable, tightly focused pieces of writing are not thick on the academic ground.

5

Children need to write (and read) frequently, and freely, in order to become adept at using complex, grammatically correct sentence structure.

Try this: Find a three-year-old and ask her to repeat this sentence word for word: "If I were rich, I would buy you the sun and the moon." I can almost guarantee that she'll say something like "I'm rich, and I'll buy you the sun and the moon." This is because she has not yet started using the subjunctive mood in her own speech, so she can't even repeat it.

Likewise, children won't start using gerund phrases and embedded adjective clauses in their sentences just because a teacher has shown them in class what they are. It's only when they've seen many of them in their reading, and done a good deal of writing, that they start creeping in, and "Jane lives behind me and is the best pitcher on our softball team and likes Popsicles, too" becomes "Jane, my Popsicle-loving friend who lives behind me, is the best pitcher on our softball team."

I've never seen this process shortened through direct teaching. On the contrary, in my experience, making kids go through endless dog and pony shows designed to teach them what an adjective clause is only makes them hostile toward writing.

Once kids have acquired these forms naturally, however, you can start talking about effective use with them. More in Part III.

6 Kids who enjoy writing are much less likely to put off required school papers and reports.

Kids excel in different ways in an English class, but usually fail the same way: They don't hand in required papers, or they hand them in so late that they lose credit.

Students who enjoy writing may go their own way on the paper—having fun using their own organization and style—and so seriously annoy an incompetent teacher. But they'll get the paper written, and all but the very weakest teachers will recognize that theirs are much better than the papers of their classmates.

7

Kids who love writing, and write frequently for pleasure, also read with better comprehension.

Reading and writing are inexorably intertwined. Children who love to read acquire a sense of written language that spills over into their writing. Children who write stories and poems and memoirs read with a much greater alertness and insight. They start to notice how an author is setting a scene, or describing a character, or using imagery.

Again, it's just like sports. Who follows those endless boring golf matches on television? Golfers. Non-golfers can barely maintain a conscious state.

8

Kids who love writing (and reading) are the students who easily excel in almost all academic subjects.

Very literate children are almost unstoppable; they are really teacher- and school-proof. Unless they are battling really serious personal problems, they'll do very well academically. And kids who are very hard-working but have never developed a habit of independent reading or writing start doing less and less well as courses get harder and harder. They lack the sophisticated understanding of language that it takes to read advanced books, or write advanced papers or reports.

9

Kids with a habit of independent, personal writing have an accessible way to work through emotional traumas.

I know Freud is somewhat in disrepute now, but I don't think anyone seriously questions that he got at least two things right: What happens to children *matters*, and somehow talking (or writing, it turns out) about past trauma helps make the trauma less toxic.

Helping your children acquire a love of writing may be the gift that keeps them stable enough to navigate safely through tumultuous times. Of course, if they are having serious trouble, you'll get professional help for them. But a habit of keeping a personal journal, or of trying to focus their experiences in stories or poetry, can be an important part of their recovery.

I can tell you that, in my experience, few teenagers have the ability to reflect upon their experiences in a way that can help them get past them. My students who have personal writing lives are among the few who can.

10 Adept, fluent writers have a wonderful advantage in most professional fields.

It seems to me that success in almost any field is much more dependent on writing ability than it used to be. Who has a private secretary in these E-mail days, to make calls, write up messages, and type up all correspondence? Or to write mission statements, long-range plans, or professional articles?

Not only can top writers do this kind of writing with one hand tied behind their back, before breakfast, but their writing will be more clearly focused, more interesting, and much more likely to persuade.

PART II:
99 WAYS TO GET KIDS TO LOVE WRITING

THE TEN MOST IMPORTANT WAYS
(If you only read ten, read these!)

1

Make sure your kids develop a love and habit of reading. This is the single most important thing you can do to ensure that they become good writers.

Think about how different writing is from speaking. When we speak, we don't have to spell the words. We don't have to worry about words that sound the same but are spelled differently, like *their, there,* and *they're.* We can help get our meaning across by raising our voice, or using gestures, or laughing or crying. We can pause for dramatic effect. We can whisper or shout.

It's much harder, and more complicated, to communicate by writing. Good writers can also whisper and shout, but they do so with varied sentence structure, with a more sophisticated vocabulary, and with imagery and metaphor. The only way to learn how to do this is through extensive reading. Avid readers acquire a familiarity with the techniques of good writers.

How do our children learn about sharing and civilized behavior? A bit of coaching can help, but what eventually turns the tide are role models. If the people children love are generous and kind and civil, sooner or later the children themselves will be also. It's the same with writing. Kids need the role model, so to speak, of reading. The more they read, the more mature a sense of language they develop.

2 **Always be encouraging about children's writing. There is something in every piece of writing that you can find to praise.**

Praise is, by far, the most effective way to motivate kids to keep writing. Ham it up. "I love the way you describe that puppy! Brown and white spots. It's so clear! I can almost see him!" Have no shame here.

As a teacher so often caught up with helping kids edit their work, I sometimes forget to do this, and then am surprised all over again when I see how effective it is. "That's a wonderful image!" I say excitedly. "It just makes the whole poem!" And then I get poem after poem after poem from that student.

3

Only offer suggestions and criticism to your kids after they've become confident, accomplished writers.

After children have really started thinking of themselves as writers, they become interested in how to make their work better. Still approach cautiously, however. "Would you like me to help you do a little editing?" ask them. "And do you think this scene would be clearer if you described the moat before you have Jonah set it on fire?"

4

Respect your children's privacy. Never read writing uninvited.

Never never, never. Not notes to their friends that fall out of their textbooks. Not notes from their friends. Not even school papers. Show interest in their writing, ask if they'd like you to read it, but never insist. And never sneak.

5 Respect your children's opinions.

Once children get the idea that their parents don't think they have anything worthwhile to say, they'll start believing that they really don't have anything of value to say to anyone. As one student said when I asked her why she never talked, or handed in much writing, in class: "Why should I think anyone in class would want to hear what I have to say," she asked, "when no one listens to me at home?"

Even when you clearly can't agree with what your children are saying, or asking, you need to hear them out respectfully—for all kinds of reasons, but also to help them become fluent, confident writers.

6 Discourage perfectionism.

One of the worst aphorisms floating around is the self-righteous statement that "if a thing's worth doing, it's worth doing right." People who try to do everything right end up either driving themselves crazy or doing nothing.

It's an especially bad mind-set for writers. Feeling that a story or essay has to be perfect not only drives out creativity and playfulness, but sometimes results in a massive writer's block.

So encourage your kids to stay loose. "Oh, just throw that underwear in the drawer," tell them. "Who cares if it gets wrinkled? It's *underwear.*"

I find that kids who grow up casually messy and a bit helter-skelter later have the patience—and ability to focus and concentrate, I think—to take infinite pains with an activity they really care about (like writing!). Their energy hasn't been diffused, and frozen, by a misguided attempt to do everything in their life by someone else's rules.

7 Don't censor your children's writing. Really objectional writing is usually just a stage.

The sweetest, nicest boys will sometimes go through stages where they write about nothing but death, or vampires, or savage murders, or all-out wars where everyone dies. The most charming girls will write love stories that have steam rising from the pages. Little children write poems that are terminally silly. Older kids write bitterly satiric essays that savage every adult in their life.

Don't worry when this happens. If you wait these stages out, they'll run their course. Be glad, and thankful, that your children share this kind of writing with you. It's quite a compliment and means that they trust you. So open your eyes wide and say, "Wow, what vivid writing!"

I think the calmer you are, the more likely they'll go on to more serious writing. What's the fun of trying to shock a parent who won't get shocked?

8

Realize that kids will have different tastes in writing, just as they do in reading. Encourage them to do the kind of writing they enjoy.

I find that young writers divide into three rough categories: those who love descriptions and imagery, and tend to write poetry and personal memoirs;

those who are sensitive to tone and voice, and tend to write character-rich stories and persuasive essays; and those who are fascinated with factual information, and tend to write complicated plots filled with accurate historical or technical detail.

It doesn't matter what kind of writing your children do. The more writing of any kind they do, the more versatile they become. By high school, all students with independent writing lives of their own are writing very good academic essays. The personal and creative writing that they've done has spilled over into their formal writing. They use detail better, and have a better sense of voice and style than students who have done only school writing. The writers who love descriptions and can create characters may do a little better in literary analysis, while the writers who love factual information tend to shine in history—but on the whole, all of these writers do very well in all academic assignments. They write circles around their classmates.

9

Don't worry about teaching grammar to kids as they are beginning to write. Most grammar knowledge is developmental, and so acquired rather than directly learned.

I explain this in much more detail in Part III, but for now keep in mind that, just as children naturally learn to speak the language they hear, they will naturally learn to write the language they read—as long, of course, as they are doing a great deal of reading. Reading is everything as far as writing grammatically goes. Why do you think children with severe hearing losses have so much trouble speaking perfectly? They don't have the input they need. Books are the input for good writing.

10

Write for pleasure yourself.

Keep a diary. Or write some poetry. Or write a family history. Or write letters. Do any kind of writing that you can easily enjoy. Not only will your enjoyment of writing make it a more attractive activity for your children, but then you'll be more knowledgeable about how writers work, and so more able to guide each child's progress.

PRESCHOOL AGE

11 **Let your children see that the stuff of their daily lives is interesting and worthwhile to talk about.**

The strongest motivation for writing is the belief that what you are saying is important. So begin the habit of listening to the small details of your children's lives when they are young and willing to talk with you.

12 **Don't try to censor or control your children's feelings.**

They can't help, after all, how they feel, and honesty and vividness in describing feelings is a mark of good writing. It's always much healthier for children to talk about feelings rather than to keep them bottled up inside.

It's tempting, when your five-year-old daughter describes her teacher as "a big doo-doo ball," to tell her that it's not nice to say that, and that she should like her teacher more. But here's the problem: Since she can't change how she feels merely because you tell her to, she'll just feel guilty or angry instead. Or she'll cover up her feelings until they make her depressed, or explosive. Instead, say something like "It must be hard to be in a classroom with a teacher you don't like. Let's talk about what we can do to try to make things work better. Maybe we should go talk to her, or..."

It's children who accept their feelings, and learn to deal with them, who later can write well about emotions. A young man in my senior class, Rich Tombeno, wrote about how close he was getting to his younger sister, but what made the essay moving and believable was his honesty in describing his earlier feelings about her: "She was always just an annoyance to me, an irritating void which sucked in all of my parents' attention. She was your typical drooling two-year-old, and seemed to follow me wherever I went..."

The wonderful image of "an irritating void which sucked in all of my parents' attention" is the eighteen-year-old equivalent of "doo-doo ball." So don't close down vivid language and feelings.

13 **Active listening is a good technique to help children expand on their ideas and experiences.**

"What did you do at nursery school?" you ask.

"We had a Halloween party!" your son says excitedly.

Now the trick is to get him to elaborate on this party, to tell you some detail, or some anecdotes about it. The basic technique of active listening is to avoid direct questions, but instead say something to show him you're a sympathetic, interested listener. So try this:

Stay quiet for a minute to see if he volunteers anything else. If he doesn't, say something like "I bet you had cookies or candy to eat." Then stay quiet to see if he takes you up on the comment.

"Our teacher said candy wasn't good for us, so we just had trail mix. I hate trail mix," he tells you.

The worst thing you can do here (as far as getting your child to keep telling you experiences) is to lecture. So resist the temptation to say, "Good for your teacher. You eat way too much candy, anyway." Instead, say something like "You must have been disappointed."

"Yeah, but Melissa gave me a cookie. She has a nice teacher."

With this kind of sympathetic attention, your child will start acquiring that wonderful ability to write with detail and emotion. So hang in.

"Melissa must be a good friend of yours..."

14

Besides respecting your children's opinions, teach them to respect other people's opinions.

Young children are prone to thinking that there is one right way to do things. While this is natural—the way the nursery school teacher shows them to put on their jackets is *the one right way*, thank you very much—you should gradually chip away at this "one right way" kind of thinking. It ultimately results in propaganda, not writing. You want your children to develop more complex ways of thinking.

So say, in a gentle way, "But I don't

like putting on my coat like that. I think I'll try another way. It's okay to do things in different ways."

You want flexible, open-minded children; that's the key for good writers (and, I think, nice people).

15 Encourage your children to engage in imaginative play.

Pretending to be fairy princesses, or spacemen, or firemen are great ways for children to gain expertise in creating stories. Not only are they creating plot, but they are also speaking in various voices, and really creating whole fictional worlds. Donate the sheets they need to make tents, and the long, flowing skirts appropriate for queens. Also keep an eye out for books that encourage this kind of play, such as the Magic Attic series, by various authors, or an action-filled fantasy such as the Narnia books, by C. S. Lewis.

16

Help your children enjoy the _sound_ of different words by making up silly sentences or rhymes with them.

A common ingredient of good writers is that they are very alive to the sound, rhythm, and cadence of words. So encourage an early interest. When your kids are giggling about "silly Billy," you can jump in and say, "Maybe he's just _chilly_...or his town is too _hilly_." Don't worry about everything making sense. You want your children to have fun with language.

17

Encourage any kind of early writing that doesn't make you crazy, such as scribbling with crayons in coloring books, drawing with colored chalk on the sidewalk, or smearing a little colorful strawberry jam on the high-chair tray.

Markers on walls and faces made me crazy, so I tried my hardest (not too successfully) to stop that. But you really want to praise and reward all other early attempts at communicating by a written form. Sure, scribbling is very primitive, but remember that your children's early attempts at speaking consisted of that lovely, gurglely jargon. That's how children learn the rhythm of a language.

18 Have more blank paper around than coloring books.

The best writing, I find, is by students who write "outside the lines," so to speak. When my children were little I used to buy up great piles of old computer paper, or blank tablets, or slightly bedraggled packs of copying paper at flea markets. They were always free to take as many sheets as they wanted, and draw great things.

The tablets are good for any time that your kids have to be sitting around waiting. I found them key especially in dentists' offices and restaurants.

19 Provide plenty of writing materials.

Have lots of paper, pencils, pens, markers, crayons, chalk—anything your children enjoy using to make marks on paper. You want communicating with written scribbles, or pictures, or words to be as natural and easy as talking for your children.

20

When your children become more verbal, and are doing more than just scribbling on paper, ask them to tell you about their writing and pictures.

Etiquette demands that you're never so gauche as to say, "What's *that?*" when presented with your three-year-old daughter's masterpiece. Instead, you should gaze thoughtfully and appreciatively at the paper and say, "Wow, that really looks interesting. Tell me all about it." Then you're not only praising early attempts, you're also encouraging her to tell you some detail, or maybe even a story, about the picture.

21

Display your children's early art and writing attempts on the refrigerator, on the kitchen walls, in your office, in letters to Grandmother—anywhere you can think of.

You do this primarily as a form of praise and encouragement, but also as a means of getting children in the habit of letting other people see and appreciate their work. It's hard for self-conscious, over-protective, or fearful writers to flourish.

22 **Read your children poetry, and buy them tapes or CD's of children's songs.**

A child who early on acquires a sense of rhythm and a love of figurative language is way ahead in the writing game. I think that exposure to lyrics and poetry also helps children learn to enjoy the sound of words—a prerequisite for any poet.

23 **Start a birthday tradition of making *When I Was Three [Four, Five, and so on]* booklets.**

These can be very simple. On the day before your preschooler turns four, say, "Let's see if we can remember some of the things that happened this year. Remember that last summer you took swimming lessons? And in the fall we got your kitten, Fluffy…"

Then get some large blank sheets of paper and write *When I Was Three* on the first one. That's your cover. Then each page could have a simple sentence dictated by your child and written by you *(I got stung by a bee)*. After you write the sentences, your child could do the illustrations.

It's very important here that you don't try to edit. Resist the temptation to say something like "Don't you think our trip to see Grandmother was more important than your getting stung by a bee?" It obviously wasn't, to your child. And half of the fun and charm of these booklets lies in the quirky, unexpected things your child thinks are memorable.

24 Encourage your children to dictate stories to you.

Many of my excellent writers remember having parents who did this. Sometimes the parents would type the stories up or sometimes just print them on construction paper. Then my students would illustrate them and have endless fun showing the books to their friends and relatives, and "reading" them.

25 Don't push your children to start writing before they are ready.

You want your children to see themselves as literate people, who enjoy reading and writing. For this to happen early, it's not necessary that they be the ones actually *doing* the reading and writing: You can be the scribe and reader. Compliment them on how well they are listening to books and telling you stories. *That* will make them feel literate.

The danger in pushing your children to read and write before they are ready is that you'll make the whole experience unpleasant for them, and make them feel dumb. That's the *worse* thing that can happen, literacy-wise.

ELEMENTARY-SCHOOL AGE

26

Encourage early writing attempts—as soon as children show they are ready—so they have a pleasant experience with writing before writing instruction starts in school.

Writing is a fairly dreary activity at many schools. Kids are assigned papers on topics that are boring to them, and are then made to write and rewrite the paper so much that all of the pride and fun in writing is drained away.

So before this happens—while your children are still young and enthusiastic about writing—try to get them writing at home.

27

Take advantage of young children's interest in how things are supposed to be done to teach them various writing forms.

Before children become ornery teenagers, most go through that lovely stage when they want to learn how to do adult things: baking, gardening, woodworking ... and *writing*. This is a good time to show them the various types.

28

Poetry writing is an easy way to start.

Since poems can be very short, a child can quickly complete a very nice piece of writing that you can get wildly excited about and hang up on the refrigerator. Show your kids how just a careful arrangement of words, and a couple of vivid adjectives, can make a nice little poem:

The soft, furry cat
Pounced!
On the little mouse.
Poor mouse.
Bad cat.

Poetry writing encourages a sense of playfulness about words and sentence structure. It helps develop an awareness of imagery and metaphor, and voice, while showing the power of writing briefly and succinctly.

29 Start with literal poems about specific experiences.

Early poetry is really just line arrangement. Take your son's description of his first-grade Halloween party ("We had lots of candy and Melissa was a witch and it wasn't fair that I didn't get a candy apple") and write everything down. With help from him, arrange the words to come out something like this:

HALLOWEEN PARTY
I was a ghost
Melissa was a witch
Lots of candy
But no candy apple
Not fair.

Then get really excited and hug him. He wrote a poem! If he enjoys this early experience, he'll gradually work up to more complex, rich language.

30 Then try silly poems.

You want your children writing silly poems because this kind of writing often blasts them loose from the kind of careful, literal writing of experience poems. Start by asking them to write down some funny words; you can do this, too. Then ask them to trade words with their friends, or with you, and make a sentence using them. Have them use the funny sentence they write as the first line of a poem.

So you'll get things like this:

The blue stupid underpants
Hit the purple car
Falling, falling
With the cat laughing

You can see that this poem, although certainly silly and somewhat meaningless, does have fresh imagery and the kind of unusual clusters of words that force new meanings. This is an aspect of very sophisticated poetry. More important, it's fun to write, and makes your children feel friendly toward poetry.

31

Tell your children that they don't need to rhyme poetry, but if they want to, they might keep in mind the guideline that rhymes should sound effortless— as if the poet was going to write that line anyway and, hey, it just happened to rhyme with the line before!

You should casually point out this kind of rhyming when you see it, either in your children's poetry or others'. Kids love "Stopping by Woods on a Snowy Evening," by Robert Frost, and it has this casual, effortless rhyming quality:

Whose woods these are I think I know
His house is in the village, though
He will not see me stopping here
To watch his woods fill up with snow.

My little horse must think it queer
To stop without a farmhouse near...

32

Keep in mind, however, that much early poetry of children, or teenagers, is trite, generic, and really pretty awful.

In spite of your efforts to get your children to write vivid poetry about specific experiences, they'll tend to slide into the kind of vague, romanticized poetry, with forced rhymes, that will sound like a fingernail on a chalkboard to you:

> *I love to play in the snow*
> *And hear the wind blow*
> *And feel cold in my toe*
> *And not feel any woe.*

Just smile enthusiastically and say, "I'm so glad you're writing poetry!" Then pick out the least awful line and say something like "And I really like the part about the wind blowing."

It's a wonderful moment when children start seeing themselves as poets. Even if they don't go on to write richer, more developed poems, they've at least gotten interested in poetry and acquired a sense of what it is. And with any luck, they've picked up a sense of imagery, tight prose, and figurative language. I really think that any poetry writing, no matter how awful, eventually spills over into more rich, vivid prose language.

33

Next, encourage diary or journal writing.

While writing poetry can make children feel proud, and feel like writers, writing about the details of their lives can put them into an intimate relationship with writing, and let them see how powerful writing is, and how much insight writing can give them into their daily experiences.

I think almost all good writers, in some way or another, write out of their own lives.

34

After your children are writing a bit more fluently, suggest newspaper writing.

Again, because children think in a literal fashion first, a journalistic style is ideal for early writers. Plus they learn to observe closely events around them, distinguish fact from opinion, and deal with quotes. Children who enjoy writing little newsletters in elementary school are also, then, in a great position to join the staff of high-school and college newspapers, where they get terrific training and practice in writing (much better, probably, than in their English classes).

35

With young children start by getting blank sheets of paper and showing them how to mark off a headline and two columns.

Then help them to write a very simple, short article. For example: "My dog Sylvester slept all morning and then ate Jenny's shoe." Write a big headline over it: "Dog Eats Shoe!" One or two more stories like that, nicely spread out, and you have a whole page. Send them out with the paper to show their friends. Write them up press badges. Hey, you're living with journalists now!

36

Offer a little editing help with their newspapers.

Since newspapers are written for public consumption (unlike diaries and poetry), suggest gently that perhaps they would like your help with the final product.

Then check Part III for tips on how to help with grammar coaching.

37

When they get a little older and are writing more independently, if you have a computer, show them how to use a newsletter template.

All computer writing programs I've ever seen have simple newsletter templates, which are just pages that are already formatted with columns and a headline space at the top. These templates are great for children's newspapers, much better than elaborate desktop publishing programs.

38

After they've been writing little newspapers for a while, show them the different kinds of news writing.

You want them to understand these distinctions not only because their newspaper writing will be better, but because they'll see that the same information can be presented and used in different ways, which will help them develop their ability to think critically.

39

Explain that in straight news writing, they should just present the facts, in descending order of importance.

The first paragraph, or lead, of a news story traditionally tells *who, how, when, where,* and *why.* Subsequent paragraphs flesh out the story a bit, and quotes liven it up.

So a simple news story would read like this:

SILVER SPOON FOUND

Jamie Sullivan's mother was surprised on Saturday morning when she found her large silver serving spoon in the hole she was digging for a tomato plant.

Her new garden was in the same place in the backyard that Jamie and his friends had used for playing with trucks and digging holes last summer. "I bet he took my spoon to dig with," Mrs. Sullivan guessed.

Jamie was not available for comment.

40

Explain that feature articles tell the story behind the news. They don't have to present the most important facts first, but can be writing in a more interesting, or creative, way.

This is a short feature article:

IS IT POSSIBLE TO REACH CHINA BY DIGGING?

This was the question that Jamie Sullivan and his friends decided to explore last August. Arming themselves with Tonka bulldozers and a variety of digging implements, they worked for two weeks digging large holes in the corner of the Sullivan backyard.

"I had heard about people digging to China, so I thought I'd give it a try," Jamie explained to this reporter. "After all, if the world is round, we should be able to go right through."

But in spite of the weeks of effort, all they got was a large hole. "And then Mrs. Sullivan made us fill it all up again," Greg Anderson, a digging friend of Jamie's, complained.

"Maybe if we'd had the right tools we could have done it," Jamie concluded.

41

Explain to your children that in editorial writing, they can give their opinion. It's common to base editorials on current news stories.

So an editorial on the silver spoon story might go like this:

KIDS' EFFORTS SHOULD
BE SUPPORTED

Last summer we all watched Jamie Sullivan and his friends digging a big hole in his backyard. They worked really hard. We didn't know it then, but they were trying to dig to China!

Unfortunately, they never found China, and one reason is that they didn't have good enough tools to dig with. Jamie finally took his mother's silver serving spoon, but it didn't work very well. The handle kind of bent, because silver is too soft.

Jamie's mother is mad that he took her spoon, but the real problem is that he didn't have a good shovel to use. Who would use a spoon when a shovel was available?

I think parents need to support their children's scientific experiments and buy them the tools they need. Finding China would have been really cool!

42

Don't expect to agree with your children's opinions.

Most adults, if writing an editorial on the silver spoon story, would talk about how irresponsible it was of Jamie to take an expensive piece of silver to dig holes in the backyard—and then not even remember to bring it back into the house! But a child editor will probably take a different slant, and that's okay. Just mildly point out that editorials work best when writers back up their opinions with facts.

43

Suggest that your children write persuasive letters when they are upset about something.

Editorial writing is great preparation for serious letter writing. Suppose your daughter's soccer team has all of its games scheduled on the worst field in town. Your daughter, or you, could call and complain, but explain to her that there is something more powerful (and, of course, formal) about a written letter. Tell her you'll help her write it.

44

Coach her a bit on exactly how to write a good persuasive letter.

Tell your daughter that good persuasive writing usually includes some facts, or logic, or anecdotes, or reference to an authority. Here's an example of a letter with all four:

27 Spruce Lane
Maple Town, MA 01788
August 23, 1998

John Reynolds
382 Main St.
Maple Town, MA 01788

Dear Mr. Reynolds:
I'm writing to tell you that my soccer team, the Blazers, has all of its games scheduled to play at Elm Street Field, the worst field in town. (Fact)

I don't think that's fair. How can we have an equal chance to win if all of our games are on the worst field? (Logic) Plus my friend Marcy Hamilton told me that her team played all of its games on Elm Street Field last year, and her team came in last in the league. (Anecdote)

My mother said that she thinks the soccer league regulations say that teams have to be treated equally. (Reference to authority) I hope you agree, and will fix this problem.

Sincerely,

Holly Meridian

Holly Meridian

45

After your children have had some experience writing about true events, in diaries or newspaper articles, suggest they try writing fiction.

I think fiction writing helps children expand their imaginations, and their ability to understand other people. Plus it's fun! It's just like playing dolls, or war; the only difference is that it's on paper, and the writer has complete control over everything. No budget difficulties over props or costumes.

46

Expect early fiction to be a thinly disguised real-life story.

Your daughter's early stories will probably read like this:

> Puff Kitten was very mad at her mother. Her mother said she had

to go to bed while it was still light out. That wasn't fair! All of her friend kittens were still up.

Most great writers, after all, start out with autobiographical fiction.

47 As your children start writing longer stories, show them how to write dialogue.

Writing dialogue helps kids develop a sense of voice and character, and at the same time ensures that their stories will be a little more developed. See what dialogue does for the kitten story—which is really just a story summary without it.

"Now," Mother Cat said with a soft purr, "it's time for you to have your bedtime lap of milk, and then curl up against me for your story."

Puff's purr died in her throat. Bedtime? While the evening sun was still warming the grass and, even more important, Tiger Stupid Cat from next door was still out playing?

"But Mother, it's too early," she protested...

Notice the two conventions of writing dialogue that you should explain. One is that you start a new paragraph every time your speaker changes—even if the speaker has only said one word. The other is that punctuation goes *inside* the quotation marks. Following these two little rules gives narrative writing a nice, professional look.

48

Explain to your children that a good way to write fiction is to take an experience they know a lot about—like playing soccer or going to camp—and then say "what if."

Most fiction is structured around a "what if" question. What if their best friend was the star of the other soccer team? Or what if, one night at camp, a real ghost came while they were telling ghost stories? The possibilities are endless.

This is a good way to encourage your children to write about what they know, while still using imaginative, fictional elements.

49

Encourage them to use a first-person narrative.

Suggest to your children that they pretend to be someone else and tell a story from that person's viewpoint. So instead of starting off like this:

Sasha felt very frightened as she listened to the ghost story. Just being around that campfire was scary enough, she thought, without hearing stories of dead campers who came back alive...

Suggest that your children start like this:

The most scary thing of all happened the last night we were at camp. We were all sitting around a campfire with just pitch-blackness all around. We couldn't even see the *trees!* Then someone started telling this awful story...

Also tell them to pretend they're telling the story to their best friend, so they don't do the kind of censoring and editing they do when they tell a story to parents or teachers. I sometimes have my classes write a story two ways, one with their parents as the audience, and one with their best friend as the audience. The differences are really comical. Do I need to tell you which stories are the most lively and interesting? And the most fun to write?

The other good thing about first-person narratives is that they give kids a sense of "voice" in fiction—something some writers never acquire.

HIGH-SCHOOL AGE

50

Suggest that your teenagers join the staff of their high-school newspaper, yearbook, or literary magazine.

These activities are great because, unlike sports teams, they don't "cut" members. Anyone can belong. Plus they'll be with a group of friends who think writing is a fun, cool thing to do. Most important, they'll be doing writing that has class-mates, rather than a teacher, for the audience.

Be very supportive of the publica-tions these groups produce. The writing will be far from professional standards, the publication dates will waver, and the whole thing may look pretty amateurish. None of this is important. What counts is that teenagers involved in these activities come to think of themselves as writers, and get invaluable experience writing for a public audience.

51 Help them think of ways to start using their writing in professional ways.

For example, I have had teenagers in my class who are fascinated with anything to do with acting or producing videos. Encourage them to write their own scripts and watch for local opportunities where they can use their talents. One high-school student produced a video for his town on conservation issues. He also worked as a summer camp counselor and helped his campers make a movie.

Support your kids' efforts to get a band together. They'll end up writing songs, performing locally, and perhaps even cutting their own tapes and CD's.

If you have teenagers interested in local issues—such as homelessness or the environment—encourage them to join advocacy or volunteer groups. There will probably be opportunities to do publicity writing, and at the very least the experience will give them lots to think and write about, on their own. Ditto for political groups.

52 **Show them how to use the Internet in writing research papers for school.**

I've been teaching kids how to write research papers for twenty-five years, but this year—the year my school district hooked the computers in the writing lab up to the Internet—was the first year we all enjoyed it.

First of all, don't get hung up on their using only the best, most respectable sites. They're not writing doctoral dissertations, just high-school history papers. What they're really learning is how to sort through information, focus it, and then write it up in a coherent way. They should also be learning what kind of information they have to footnote, or use an internal citation for (direct quotes, opinion, or information that is not common knowledge to someone familiar with the field), and how to write up a bibliography.

The Internet makes this all much

easier. First, show them how to open two screens on their computer monitor: one for the Internet and one for a word-processing notes file. Then, as soon as they find information, have them either copy and paste, or save the whole file into their notes file. Be sure they have the URL (the http:www code that is on the top of the screen for each site) in their notes file as well, since they'll need it for their bibliography. They can just copy and paste it in.

After they've collected enough information, have them open two files again, their notes file and a new word-processing file for their paper. Then they can have all of their information right next to them on the screen as they write, and they can paste in direct quotes without even retyping them. And they can cut and paste those URL numbers right into their bibliography.

If they are also using books and periodicals as sources, suggest that they type these notes into their computer as well.

Although this may seem complicated to you, it doesn't to kids, all of whom are born with a computer gene these days. They'll quickly think up even more shortcuts and variations and, with any luck, have a little fun doing this most dreaded of high-school assignments.

53 Coach them a bit on writing their college application essay.

The college application essay gives you an opportunity to talk about what good writing is. Tell them that a good college essay is fresh and honest, that it doesn't have to be about a tragic or marvelous event, but it does have to give a little insight into them as people.

A number of years ago I had one of the best wrestlers in the state in my English class. He wrote a wonderful essay about the time he was a school bus monitor in fifth grade. The class bully (who wore a "gas station shirt") was on his bus, and one day the bully got off at his, the monitor's, best friend's stop—and it *wasn't* the bully's stop. The writer agonized over what to do: leave his duties on the bus or leave his friend unprotected. He finally decided to get off the bus also, and then managed to talk the bully out of fighting. He saw the point of his essay as showing that peaceful ways, if at all possible, are always best; I saw his essay as showing what an extraordinarily sweet and conscientious kid he was.

When he got accepted at all of the colleges he applied to, everyone else thought it was because of his decent grades and wonderful wrestling talent. And maybe it was. But I bet that college essay didn't hurt, either.

54. Don't demand that your teenagers get all top grades in school.

Some students drive themselves to get top grades, and if your teenager is one of them, that's fine. Stand back and admire. But if you have a teenager who would rather take some time to smell the roses—and do some creative projects—I think that's fine, too. Don't push these kids into honors classes and insist that they get all A's. Good writing takes time and emotional energy; students who are under intense parental pressure won't have this kind of energy available. Nor will they develop the self-confidence and courage that really wonderful writing requires.

Actually, I find that kids under great

parental pressure don't even have the motivation or energy to do well on regular school assignments. The rule of thumb is that as parental pressure increases, the amount and quality of work decreases.

You should always be warmly supportive of your children, but as they become teenagers, direct pressure becomes less and less effective. So admire their work, but don't stand over them with arms folded supervising their every move. You might get a short-term gain doing this, but there's no "might" about the long-term loss.

WRITING-FRIENDLY ACTIVITIES AND ROUTINES

55

Be a note-writing family.

Have a family message center—preferably by the phone—with plenty of paper and pens. Use any excuse to leave your children notes, but try not to make all of the notes be directions—like "Dirty dishes go in the dishwasher. Thank you. The Management." Instead,

or in addition, leave notes compliment-
ing your daughter on her soccer game,
or wishing your son luck on his English
test.

56 **If you are getting a family computer,
consider getting a laptop rather than
a desktop one.**

I think laptops are much more user-
friendly. Children can curl up on the
couch with them. Or they can take them
to their rooms when they want to write
private stories or diary entries. And, as a
short adult, I can testify that a regular-
size computer on a regular-size desk isn't
even comfortable for me to use.

57 **If you can afford it at all, consider
getting a laptop solely for the use of
each of your older children.**

I know this sounds hopelessly extrava-
gant, but stripped-down laptops are
starting to be available in the thousand-
dollar range. Plus you should be able to
get a good used laptop for even less. If
you have an athlete, think what you
spend on sports equipment, fees, and

summer camps. Or just figure out what you spend on video rentals and cable television over a year's time. I think a laptop is a bargain next to those expenses.

A personal laptop is wonderful for access and privacy. It's always available—no one else is ever spending hours doing a research paper on it—and no matter how careful you are to honor your children's privacy, I think they are always conscious, when using a family computer, that other people could read their writing. We are a family that is very respectful of one another's privacy, but when my daughter got her own laptop for college, the first thing she did was to password-protect it—as my husband found out when he tried to install some software for her.

58 Keep a family history, with pictures and some narration.

This would be a wonderful project to do during the last drawn-out days of the Christmas vacation. Gather together snapshots that you've kept of the year's activities, and buy a large scrapbook.

Have your children help you select the best snapshots, and then write a two- or three-sentence description of what each picture shows. You could type out the descriptions and paste them in the scrapbook, right along with the photographs.

As your children get older, you might encourage them to keep a history of their own, in addition to the family one.

59 **As a slumber party or birthday party activity, suggest that the children write group stories, and offer a prize for the best one.**

I do this in class all the time, and the kids really like it.

First put the children in groups of three or four. Give everyone a few slips of paper and say something like "Now take the first slip of paper and write down your favorite color. Now take the next one and write down your favorite food." Or sport, or holiday, or anything. Then put all of the slips in a big box and have the children draw out as many as they put in.

Now give them a little pad of paper,

and tell them to make up an "I" sentence using all of the words. So you might get "I love pizza but was really grossed out when Marnie brought one with blue cheese to our soccer game." Have the children write their sentence on the pad and then pass the pad around to the friend on the left in their group.

When all of the children have a pad of paper with a sentence on it that they didn't write, tell them to write for five minutes and continue the story. Then have them pass the pad again to the person on their left and continue with five-minute writing sessions until everyone in the group has written on each story. (With younger children you might want to go to two- or three-minute writing periods.) Then read the stories out loud and ask them to choose the best.

This gets kids having fun with writing, it lets them see how their friends write, and, at the end, it gets them evaluating writing.

60
Look on the Internet for writing sites for children.

I've found a few that look pretty promising. Some seem pretty selective about what they publish, and others seem to publish almost everything. But, at any rate, your kids will get to see other children's writing—and writing that is published! Plus, with any luck, your kids will want to submit their writing also.

These are the ones I've found. I'm sure there are lots more:

www.stonesoup.com   This is the Internet site for the excellent children's magazine *Stone Soup*. It's filled with high-quality children's writing, and has a page with guidelines for submissions.

www.kidstory.com   This site is called *Kids Writing for Kids*, and children can submit poetry or stories, or write a story on-line in a box and submit it right then. It looks to me like they publish almost everything, so this is the site for young writers who need a boost to their self-confidence.

www.realkids.com/club.htm   This is the Young Writers Clubhouse site. It offers advice on how to write, how to get published, and even has a young writer's critique group. This looks like a great site for children who have already had some success with writing.

61

Encourage your children to submit their best work to contests or children's magazines.

A number of my very good high-school writers told me that they had been published in a children's magazine. I think this is the equivalent of a soccer player getting to play in a national tournament. It's very exciting, and makes young writers see themselves as real authors. A good source for lists of editors willing to look at the work of children or teenagers is *To Be a Writer: A Guide for Young People Who Want to Write and Publish* by Barbara Seuling (Twenty-First Century Books, 1997).

Besides encouraging your children to submit to national magazines, I'd encourage submissions to local outlets, like a school literary magazine or a town newspaper, where their work has an excellent chance of acceptance.

62

Encourage your children to publish their own work.

Self-publishing is the in-thing to do nowadays, in this age of computers and laser printers. Besides publishing their own newspapers, your children could publish little books of stories or poetry. And computers aren't even necessary. Tell them that handmade books are even more special.

These books would make great gifts for relatives and friends—or they could have a book fair and sell them to sympathetic neighbors (whose children sell *you* Girl Scout cookies and greeting cards). Invest in one of those long staplers that are made for stapling booklets.

63

Keep in mind that real writers have different writing routines.

Some writers work on only one project at a time; others work on this for a while, and then spend a little while on that. Some writers finish almost everything they start; others leave a large number of barely started and half-finished manuscripts in their wake.

Kids are the same way. Some will binge on one kind of writing; others will drift from fiction writing to poetry to journal writing. Some want to finish everything. Others finish nothing. And that's okay. You just want them writing.

WHAT TO LOOK FOR IN A SCHOOL

Note: I realize that parents can't get schools made to order, but I do think that parents have more influence than they think. Most school administrators want parents on their side. I'm listing below the elements of a writing-friendly school so you'll know what to look for, and what aspects of writing education to encourage.

64

Look for warm, nurturing teachers.

This is the most important school tip. A loving teacher can coax writing out of the most recalcitrant student, and can elicit wonderfully developed pieces of writing from more advanced writers. Plus a teacher who really cares about her students is much more likely to change the curriculum to suit the needs of her particular children. In writing, as in most of education, treating children as individuals gets the best results.

65 Look for a school with a low student-teacher ratio.

The fewer students a teacher has, the more time she has to read student writing. Most public school teachers have far too many students to do any kind of adequate job with writing. How can a teacher who is already stretched too thin with multiple preparations, students who need intensive one-on-one help, rapidly changing state assessment requirements, and endless meetings and professional development courses have the time to spend twenty or thirty hours a week responding thoughtfully to student writing? She can't and she won't.

So demand that your school district restrict elementary-school classes to twenty students, and total teaching loads for secondary English teachers to eighty students and four classes.

66

Look for schools that give teachers a good deal of academic freedom.

Excellent writing isn't a skill that can be produced on demand. Every child and every teacher is different, and the teacher who feels free to try different teaching techniques and various assignments will have better luck. You want your children in a school that encourages this kind of innovation.

67

Look for schools that support independent reading for students.

Since a habit of reading is so critical for writing success (and academic success in general), look for schools that make independent reading a part of the curriculum. Most children need a good deal of encouragement and support to develop a habit of independent reading; parents *can* provide this support, but the job is infinitely easier if the schools are helping.

The worst thing a school can do, as far as reading goes, is to require kids to read one assigned book after another. With an assigned book hanging over their heads, few kids read anything else—and many don't even read the assigned book. They ask a friend what was in it, watch the video, or read the *Cliff Notes*. What you want to find is a school that assigns *independent* reading, and then monitors the reading by requiring students to keep journals and attend conferences or book club meetings—or by some other means the student finds.

68

Look for schools that emphasize creative writing.

I'm convinced that students don't learn to write well doing only, or primarily, school-essay type writing. You know the kind of writing I mean: the essays that have an introduction, a thesis, maybe quotes and outside sources. This is the equivalent of painting by numbers. The finished picture might look okay (although never dazzling), but the artist learned little in doing the painting.

It's only when kids are turned loose and encouraged to do a great deal of writing that is exciting and meaningful to them that they start to acquire real fluency and a sophisticated sense of language. Once that happens, it's easy to teach them conventional formats.

69 Look for a school that treats students like real authors.

You want a school that displays student writing, that has activities like "authors" breakfasts—when parents are invited to read their children's writing—and that supports student publications like newspapers and literary magazines. Some schools do really wonderful things like having local children's authors in occasionally, or teaming students up with senior citizens in joint writing activities.

The key is to look for a school that seems to respect the individuality and differing talents of young writers.

70 Be wary of schools that make extensive use of rubrics for writing.

Rubrics are a system for evaluating writing. The idea is that you look at a sixth grader's story, for example, and say, "Well, on a scale of one to ten, the use of detail in this story is a three, the transitions between paragraphs is a five, the dialogue is a six," and so on.

While this kind of analysis can be useful in very limited situations (such as individual testing by a trained clinician looking for learning disabilities), I don't think it's useful in normal classroom situations. It results in cookie-cutter writing—stories all written to the same pattern. Donald Murray, a retired University of New Hampshire professor and author of many books on writing, told me that there was only one rule of writing: Do whatever works. He was incredulous and dismayed when I told him about the growing use of rubrics in elementary and secondary classrooms.

The worst thing about rubrics, however, is that their use discourages young writers. No writing is ever good enough; some area is always marked down. In reality, of course, a well-written story develops some aspects at the expense of others. A riveting suspense story sometimes works better without much description. Great villains tend to be one-dimensional. A story written to get all ten's in a rubric evaluation would probably be unwieldy and overwritten.

The use of rubrics means kids are continually trying to write to another's standards, rather than developing their own critical faculties.

71

If you must have your children in schools where writing is poorly taught, or not taught at all, look for the teachers there that at least do no harm.

It's my own feeling that writing is generally the worst-taught subject in school. And I think this is because very few elementary or secondary teachers have independent writing lives themselves; even English teachers tend to dislike writing. Imagine if most football coaches disliked football—or if most medical school professors hated the sight of a hospital. I think at least a degree of enthusiasm and expertise in a subject is necessary for teaching it to someone else.

How can you tell if a teacher is doing harm? Watch your children. If your son is cheerfully doing assignments—even though they seem ridiculous to you—he's probably okay. Some teachers can even make rubrics and endless grammar exercises fun. Maybe your son isn't learning much, but at least he isn't being harmed. But if he starts to dread writing and puts off assignments, he's signaling a problem. Try to find out exactly what is going on. Ask for a conference. If it appears that the writing instruction is at fault, emphasize that the way writing is being taught isn't working for your child; indeed, it's making him hate writing. Ask what you can do to help the situation, and ask the teacher what he or she will do.

If the teacher isn't at all open to this kind of dialogue, consider your options. If your son is surviving the year pretty well anyway, you may want to let it slide. Maybe he'll get a more encouraging, exciting teacher next year. But if he's becoming depressed, or rebellious, or hostile to school, I'd go to the principal and ask for a teacher change. Even if you don't get the change, at least you've put the principal on notice that this teacher, or this writing program, is unsatisfactory. It's only when many parents complain that administrators are willing to go through the hard work of changing curriculum or firing a teacher.

KIDS WITH SPECIAL DIFFICULTY WRITING

72

Try to figure out exactly what the difficulty is.

Some children have such poor small motor control that the physical act of writing is very difficult. Very visual children are often slow to come to reading, and that holds them back in writing as well. Kids with emotional problems are often terrified of writing because they think their anger or despair is so huge and overwhelming that it has to be kept hidden; they don't dare let it out on a page. A learning disability can ensure that early writing attempts are so chaotic and unreadable that the child gets discouraged and doesn't want to try any more. Or you may have children who have been taught writing in such a hostile or repressive manner that they now simply hate everything about writing.

Your first step in dealing with any of these problems is to figure out exactly what is going on

73

First, assess how much time your child spends reading. If your child does very little reading, assume that's the basis of much, or all, of the writing problem.

Kids who do very little reading use as their model spoken, rather than written, language. This means their sentence structure is loose and rambling, and their writing is often filled with run-on sentences. They mix up homonyms like *blue* and *blew* because the words sound alike, and their reference is spoken language. Their vocabulary is rudimentary, and they often write with a curiously detached voice, almost as if they're describing actions on a screen.

The solution to this problem is, of course, to get them reading. I'd do this before anything else, just as I'd give a hearing aid to a hearing-impaired child before I'd really start working on speech therapy. When children start avidly reading, their writing usually improves dramatically.

74

A child with poor handwriting should be allowed to print or to use a computer.

I've had too many students tell me that they hated writing in elementary school because the teacher was always complaining about their handwriting. This is so unnecessary. Kids don't write poorly on *purpose*. They have trouble with fine motor skills—or sometimes they are very bright and think much too fast for their handwriting to keep up with them. A number of students have told me that a computer finally freed them to write well. It also frees them to be able to show off their work to their friends.

75

Children who can't spell should be taught spelling survival strategies.

Spelling is a funny thing. There's so much emotion surrounding it—if you want to get in a raging argument, just mention that you believe in "creative" or "invented" spelling—and yet it seems to me to be the one element of writing that is least amenable to teaching. Children who spell well are kids who read well—of course—but then also have very good visual *and* auditory processing abilities. Highly developed literary abilities can't compensate for a poor visual memory or poor auditory discrimination when it comes to spelling.

So teach your poor spellers to use the spell check on their computer, and encourage them to recruit proofreaders to help them edit really important writing. Make sure they have a little paperback dictionary they can easily carry with them. When they ask you how to spell something, just *tell* them.

It's fashionable to blame poor spelling on a lack of phonics teaching, but I haven't found that to be the case. The hallmark of a poor speller is often that he spells *everything* phonetically—so *creche*, for example, becomes "cresh."

Most important, don't let poor spellers think they are dumb just because they frequently misspell common words. I don't think spelling has anything to do with intelligence. In fact, sometimes very intelligent children spell poorly simply because they are impatient with what they see as unimportant details.

76

Children who make many grammatical errors should be surrounded with *any* kind of reading material—comics, magazines, newspapers, cereal boxes, baseball cards—*anything*.

Stephen Krashen, a University of Southern California researcher, points out in his book *The Power of Reading: Insights from the Research* that children with a habit of independent reading will reach acceptable levels of literacy on their own. They acquire a sense of written language that can't be directly taught.

I've tried every trick I know—from teaching the diagramming of sentences, to playing grammar games, to having kids make up grammar exercises, to using grammar books—to get kids to use respectable sentence structure. Avid readers, who are already using sophisticated grammatical structures in their writing, can quickly learn to identify gerunds and adjective clauses and dangling participles—everything—while poor readers can't reliably find even the subject or predicate.

If you don't know how to get your

children reading, you might read one of my other books: *Parents Who Love Reading, Kids Who Don't; Keeping Kids Reading;* or *99 Ways to Get Kids to Love Reading.*

77 **Try to find writing activities that will motivate your poor writers to do some pleasure writing.**

I know that this is difficult, but, again, practice is everything. I know one learning-disabled young man (in a ten-page paper of his I counted a hundred spelling errors) who became an excellent writer after he got his own laptop computer and started using the Internet. Between writing his own Web page, posting messages in the Usenet section, and writing and answering E-mail, he wore out two paperback dictionaries—and learned how to write.

Perhaps you can get your sports-loving children to write up their games for the local paper, or even just keep a scrapbook themselves, with pictures and written descriptions of their games. Encourage them to keep lists of their hockey cards, or the game stats of their baseball games. You want them to do anything that involves putting pen to paper—or hands to keyboard.

78 Help as little as possible with school writing.

Here's why. Many children who have initial difficulty writing start feeling like they are really terrible writers, and really can't write at all. It's very important that they start taking responsibility for assigned writing themselves, and they won't do that if you are always there, pushing them on and organizing everything for them. Even young children should feel like *they* are the ones in charge of their writing.

So be available but not intrusive. Don't keep track of the papers they have due. Don't keep reminding them about assignments. You get a short-term gain with this kind of help, but a long-term loss (i.e., they get this paper done but are even less likely to do the next one completely on their own).

Most children, when the need arises, will start writing independently. And it's only when that happens that they become engaged with their writing, and start to feel empowered by it.

79

If your children bring a paper to you and ask for your help, be very respectful of them as the author.

Ask your children what they would like your help with. Spelling, perhaps? Punctuation? Organization? The idea is to keep ownership of the paper with them. Don't take it over.

Then sit down with them and make only the suggestions that they have asked for. Remember, you're not trying to finish up with the best possible paper. You're trying to help your children develop as writers, and for that to happen your children need to be in control of their writing. Of course, you could rewrite the paper so that it would be much better, but then it wouldn't be *their* paper. Less is more here.

In the long run, too much parental (or teacher) help on papers results in lack of self-confidence and real writer's block with students.

80

When children stop writing altogether, it's often because they are struggling with emotional issues.

Depressed, or fearful, or traumatized children can have an extraordinarily difficult time writing. I think they are afraid that others will find out things about them that they don't want known, for one thing, and I also think they are afraid that *they* will have to face things they don't want to face, if they write them down.

So be very gentle and encouraging. Being harsh and demanding just makes them more fearful, and so more unable to write. See if they'll dictate an assignment or story to you. Try to create lots of opportunities for little daily bread-and-butter-type writing tasks, such as leaving messages, answering notes, etc. You're trying to break through a very real writing block. And you might try encouraging them to write some poetry—I've had some pretty good luck doing that.

Finally, of course, if your children continue being sad, or angry, or withdrawn, get professional help for them.

FLUENT, INDEPENDENT WRITERS

81

Realize that if your children become especially interested in writing, and are good at writing, you may have to be the one to act as their writing mentor.

Children who are athletes, or artists, or musicians, or even scientists can usually be provided with good teachers, either privately or through their school system. But children who are talented writers are often out of luck. Few teachers—even English teachers—have had much training in anything other than analytical writing, and few communities are awash in writing teams or writing bands.

By the time your children get to high school, there may be a group of students interested in writing who put out a literary magazine, and later there are numerous writing workshops and support groups for college students and adults. But initially, you may be the only resource your children have.

So in this section I'll try to coach you a bit so you can act as an effective mentor.

82

Start giving more complete feedback as your children become better writers.

This point comes when your children are writing fluently and easily, and have started to develop an independent writing life of their own, apart from school and from you. When this happens, you can start having more serious discussions with them about the quality of their work—what's good about it, and how they can make it better.

83

Look for each child's particular strength.

Writing is at least as rich and complex a field as music or sports. You wouldn't try to make a young woman with a gorgeous soprano voice play the trombone, would you? Or try to take a natural pitcher and make him a hockey goalie? It's okay to have individual talents. The trick is to help your children identify their particular strengths.

84

Visual, artistic children tend to write with a good deal of imagery and vivid detail.

These children are pretty easy to spot. They often loved myths and fantasies as young children—because of the almost metaphorical detail, I think—and, when older, are thoughtful, mediative kinds of kids. Sometimes they are great outdoorsman and spend hours fishing or hiking (and storing away lovely nature images for later use). Remember my student Rich Tombeno, who used that great image of his sister as "an irritating void which sucked in all of my parents' attention"? He's an outdoorsman who also wrote this:

> But now society seems like a flood, something paradoxically deadly. I try to stay afloat in a current of phony attitudes and cheeriness, but I can't. I am learning how to bob along the surface, gasping for breath between each crashing wave that pulls me down again. My parents call to me from somewhere and tell me to swim, to have fun, that I'm a freak because I don't go out with girls on Saturday

nights. They say that I need to socialize, but they don't know I'm drowning as it is.

I think his imagery is breathtaking, as good as anything I've seen from established authors. (And he's happily ensconced in a college in the mountains now, minoring in writing, and making lots of friends who also love the outdoors.)

85

With these visual writers, stress that effective imagery is fresh, and compels a richer understanding.

I tell my students that there is a huge cache of images that most people pull from: "Dark as night" is one, or "cold as ice." The problem is that when you use imagery like this, your reader's mind just passes right over it; it's been so overused it no longer carries any real meaning.

This snippet from a poem by one of my high-school juniors, Rachel Ropeik, shows the power of unexpected, unusual imagery:

> *She is open and vulnerable*
> *like a woman emerging wet from a*
> *shower—*
> *Cold and Alone and needing help.*

Wrap her in a towel of security and help
her through the life she still has
Calm her shivering soul with support
Give her the bathrobe and slippers of
your love.
Isn't that lovely?

86 Encourage rewriting when meaning is unclear.

I find that visual writers, while often dazzling me with their descriptions, sometimes confuse me with their plots. The action is sometimes a bit boring to them, and little details like moving characters from one place to the next occasionally get overlooked.

But luckily I've also found that visual writers are usually the most interested in rewriting, perhaps because of their thoughtfulness and openness.

87 Suggest that visual writers read authors who enrich their writing with interesting detail, descriptions, and images.

Almost all good poets fit this description (especially e. e. cummings, some early

Yeats, W. H. Auden, all of the Romantics, and many contemporary poets), but there are many prose writers who do as well. Some books that come readily to mind are *Like Water for Chocolate*, by Laura Esquivel, *Midnight in the Garden of Good and Evil*, by John Berendt, *A Prayer for Owen Meany*, by John Irving, *Sassafras, Cypress & Indigo*, by Ntozake Shange, and anything by Annie Dillard.

88

You may have to offer special support to these rich, detailed-filled writers, since few teachers recognize the possibilities of this kind of style.

I find that these writers get the least support in regular school classes. Many teachers dismiss their early writing as vague and wordy, and by the time they can write the kind of wonderful poetry I've quoted above, they're in high school—and few high schools offer courses in poetry writing, or even in creative writing in general. Also, these writers are less likely to distance themselves from their writing by the use of irony or sarcasm. Their writing is usually intensely personal, which makes them very vulnerable to harsh teacher judgments.

So look for school-based literary magazines—perhaps you can help start one—or outside opportunities for showcasing your child's work. It's important that these kids get validation of themselves as good writers.

89

Very verbal children do well creating exciting narrators and sharply defined characters.

The ability to write with a distinctive, engaging voice is the special province of these authors. Here's a sample piece of writing from one of my sophomores, Alyssa Galeros:

> It was freedom, it was joy, it was the first day of summer vacation. I was feeling pretty damn cool strolling along the crowded cement path of Canobie Lake amusement park; I had lost the parental units, had my allowance in my pocket, and my best friend by my side. We were the untouchables, we were slick, we were hip: we were thirteen.

Notice the assured tone throughout, and the comic, self-mocking irony in "we were slick, we were hip: we were thirteen." It's a wonderful piece of writing.

90

You can help these very verbal writers explore different kinds of narrations.

Point out that in a traditional third-person narration, the narrator can easily move the reader around to different scenes, and can explicitly describe exactly what is going on. For example:

> Micah and his brother Josh got in another big fight after school on Tuesday. Although they fought casually, and frequently, this fight had an extra tone of bitterness to it. For the first time, it was over a girl.

A first-person narration of the same scene offers more warmth and intimacy, but less information:

> Josh, that creep, started trying to move in on Stacy, my girlfriend. I couldn't believe it! Fine. If he

wants to fight again, we'll fight again. I always beat that little jerk anyway.

In addition to these two fairly classic techniques, there is a third, called, variously, a stream-of-consciousness narrative, an "over the shoulder" narrative, or a modified first-person narrative. The idea is that the third-person narrator tells the story from inside, rather than outside, of a character. So it sounds something like this:

Who would think your own brother would be a Judas? Micah slammed his locker door in fury. Stacy was the sun, the moon, the one dazzling light in his otherwise bleak life. And then Josh, that little creep, decides to move in! Micah wasn't going to take this lying down.

Notice how the narrator here is describing the situation solely through the viewpoint of Micah. Presumably, Stacy isn't *really* the sun and the moon, but she seems so to Micah, even though it's something he wouldn't articulate in a first-person narrative. This is a pretty sophisticated narration to handle, but, if done correctly, can maintain the warmth and intimacy of a first-person narrative without sacrificing the flexibility found in a third-person one.

91 **Sometimes, with these writers, you need to suggest that they describe their characters and setting a bit more completely.**

Sometimes very verbal children don't notice visual detail. Encourage them to enrich their writing by describing setting, the appearance of characters, etc. Explain to them that they don't need long, involved descriptions that would slow down their narration; often a few telling details will do. If they describe a villain as having "ice gray eyes and pale, slicked-back hair," the reader not only gets a visual picture of the man, but a sense of his character as well.

92 **Look for books with interesting narrative techniques for them to read.**

For example, you might want to recommend *Pride and Prejudice*, by Jane

Austen, for its wonderful irony; *Ellen Foster,* by Kaye Gibbons, for the tragic-comic tone and the interesting way the child narrator switches between the present and the past; *Catch-22,* by Joseph Heller, for its absurd humor and social satire; *Ordinary People,* by Judith Guest, for the over-the-shoulder narrator who switches between the son's and the father's viewpoint—as well as a host of others. Even popular fiction—mysteries especially—often have lively, engaging narrators. Or simply encourage them to be aware of the narrator in whatever fiction they are currently reading.

93

These students who are so adept at different tones sometimes have trouble with teachers who don't appreciate irony or comedy.

Students like this sometimes have a very hard time writing dull, ordinary school essays. It's so much more fun to add a little twist to it—a bit of sarcasm or a ridiculous detail—anything to liven it up. Many teachers really enjoy this, but there are some others (dull, stick-in-the-mud types) who think your children are making fun of *them*—which, of course, your kids would never, never do.

I find these funny, articulate verbal students usually have a good amount of self-confidence, so I wouldn't worry too much about their occasional teacher run-ins. Sit back and enjoy the show.

94

Some kids aren't especially strong either in descriptions or narrations, but are wonderful storytellers.

I find these are students who have a good facility for absorbing and making sense out of great amounts of information. They also tend to develop passionate interests, such as science fiction, or sports, or war, or relationships. If they keep on writing, and especially if they can manage to make their interests intelligible and exciting to a general public, they may go on to be very successful commercial writers—like Tom Clancy or John Grisham or Jean Auel.

95

Encourage these young storytellers, even when their first stories are interminable and very difficult to follow.

Rome wasn't built in a day, and I find that the early writing of these kids isn't as engaging or fun to read as the writing of my other students. They write in copious detail about spaceships or wars or long, tumultuous relationships. But that's okay. They're learning how to bring together lots of information. Insight can come later.

96

As they write more, start suggesting that they add some description, or a narrator with a bit of personality.

I find these students very amenable to coaching. It's not that they don't want to enrich their writing; they just tend not to think of doing it on their own. Explain about imagery to them. Show them different narrators. Explain that vivid characterizations and descriptions help a reader better follow the intricacies of their plots.

97 **The trick is to find good storytellers for them to read who also have a lively, developed style.**

And there are many of them. Stephen King writes very vividly and movingly about life in little New England towns. You might point out to your children that the reason his horror stories work so well is because everything in them—except the horror part—is so believable. Piers Anthony writes fantasy and science fiction filled with fresh, unexpected detail and engaging narrators. Rosamunde Pilcher's novels, especially her later ones, capture the sweep of life in England over the last forty years while telling complex, riveting family stories. Maeve Binchy does the same thing in Ireland. All of these authors are compelling storytellers, but also very rich, textured writers.

98 **Generally, these storytelling writers do pretty well in school, since their grasp of factual knowledge endears them to their teachers.**

Occasionally when I have these practical students in class, they get annoyed at some poet or novelist who seems too romantic or *vague* to them. Sometimes they get impatient with a search for imagery or layers of meaning. Let's get on with the story! But, on the whole, they are wonderful students.

FINALLY

99

Keep your perspective. Having children who are wonderful writers (and readers) isn't as important as having children who are good people.

It's very easy when we're so concerned about our children doing well in school and in their own independent reading and writing projects to agree with them that they don't have time for the little kindnesses and duties of life—like visiting their grandparents or helping us with the dishes. I'm afraid that when we do this, though, we're in danger of producing self-absorbed, entitled children.

My own opinion is that it's even more important for gifted writers to be people of integrity and compassion—since they can wield such power and influence.

PART III:
TEN EASY TIPS
FOR TEACHING GRAMMAR

I teach an advanced senior writing course, and I've found that the great majority of these students are great readers, pretty good writers, and know no formal grammar at all. Years of doing grammar exercises in elementary and middle school seem to have washed right over them. They *write* grammatically, for the most part, but can't do any final editing since they can't pick out pronoun disagreements or problems with sentence construction—or any of the other little errors that can slip through in the writing even of excellent writers.

They need a knowledge of formal grammar to do this. What follows are some of the tricks I've picked up, over the years, to give them and my other students this knowledge.

The most important thing I've learned, which I know I'm emphasizing again and again, is that grammar constructions can't be directly taught until the students have acquired those constructions in their writing. I know this sounds backward, but I've tried every-thing—*everything*—to teach them earlier. It can't be done. Kids have to have a sense of sophisticated sentence structure before they can understand the concept of subordinate clauses or noun phrases or infinitives.

But, again, the good news is that all kids who avidly read acquire this sophisticated sense of language and write pretty well without any knowledge of grammar at all. So teach your children some grammar so they can do the final polish to their writing, but keep in mind that the most important thing you can do, grammar-wise, is to nurture a love of reading in them.

1 **Don't try to give formal grammar lessons, unless you have an extraordinarily receptive, eager-to-learn child. Teach grammar in conjunction with your child's writing.**

Children simply absorb grammar rules better when you're talking about their own writing, rather than some sentences on a worksheet. They don't care about the worksheet sentences, which are almost always stunningly boring, but they do care about stories and poems they've written themselves.

2

Call your help "editing" and always offer it as a favor, not a requirement.

So do say: "I love that poem you wrote. Would you like me to help you edit it a bit so it looks perfect?" Don't say: "You can't turn in that paper with all of these mistakes! Come here. I'll show you how to fix them."

When you help your children, be very respectful. It's their work, tell them, and you're just offering suggestions. They don't have to take your suggestions. They have the final say on their own work.

3

Use correct grammatical terms when helping your children with their writing, but do it casually. Don't try to make them learn these terms. Let them pick them up naturally.

At some point children need to know the parts of speech, and also such terms as *phrases* and *clauses*. Starting when your children are young, work these terms into your comments. "I love the adjectives you use to describe that castle!" say enthusiastically. Or "Your action verbs are so good! I can just see how that horse is running around."

Here's a quick review of the parts of speech:

Nouns name a person, place, or thing—like *apple* or *Paris*.

Pronouns take the place of a noun—like *he* or *they*.

Verbs show action—*scream, jump*—or a state of being—*is, were*.

Adjectives describe nouns—like *big* or *cowardly*.

Adverbs describe verbs, adjectives, or other adverbs—*very* or *quickly*.

Prepositions show place or position—as in *over* the river and *through* the woods.

Conjunctions connect words, phrases, or clauses—*because, and, since, when*.

Interjections show strong emotion—*Wow!*

Your children also need to know the terms that describe each word's job, or position, in a sentence:

The predicate slot is always filled by a verb, and it tells the main action, or does the main connecting, in a sentence. So in the sentence *Tom sent roses*, the verb *sent* is the predicate, because sending something is the main action of that sentence. In *Tom is smart*, the verb *is* is the predicate, because it links *Tom* and *smart*.

The subject is usually a noun or a pronoun (but occasionally a verbal; more later) and does the action. *Tom* is the subject, since he's sending the roses.

The direct object receives the action. Since the roses are what is being sent, *roses* is the direct object.

Some sentences have indirect objects. In the sentence *Tom sent Henrietta roses*, *Henrietta* is the indirect object. Indirect objects follow the predicate and have "to" understood in front of them. *Tom sent (to) Henrietta roses.*

Besides predicates, prepositions can take objects. In *over the river and through the woods* both *river* and *woods* are objects of prepositions. A preposition and its object make up a prepositional phrase.

The easiest parts of speech to mix up are adjectives and adverbs. To keep them straight, use the apple test. Apple is a noun, right? So put the questionable word in front of "apple" and see if it makes sense. A *big* apple? Fine. A *pretty* apple? That's okay, too. Big and pretty are adjectives. How about a *very* apple? Nope. Very is an adverb. Notice that since adverbs—which are really your multipurpose part of speech—can describe adverbs, adjectives, or even other adverbs, you can say a very pretty apple, because *very* can describe the adjective *pretty*. But not the noun *apple!*

Verbs get a little complicated also, because they sometimes do the job of other parts of speech. For example, sometimes verbs will act like nouns and be the subject or object of a sentence (*Running* is fun), and then we call them gerunds. When verbs act like adjectives (a *rolling* stone), we call them participles. When verbs have the word "to" in front of them *(to roll)*, we call them infinitives. Infinitives are the all-purpose verbal forms. They can act like nouns and be subjects or objects *(To roll a stone is fun)*, or like adjectives *(I want a stone to roll)*, or like adverbs *(He ran to get home quickly)*.

I wouldn't worry too much about these forms early on, though. If your children can acquire a familiarity and ease with the parts of speech I listed above, and the idea of subjects, predicates, and objects, they'll be ahead of ninety-nine percent of their classmates.

4. **Don't try to teach sentence structure until complex sentences start showing up in your child's writing.**

What are complex sentences? Here's a brief review:

A clause is your main sentence building block. A clause has a subject and a predicate.

A simple sentence is made up of one independent clause: *The girl made a fortune on her lemonade stand.* Note that the prepositional phrase *(on her lemonade stand)* doesn't turn a simple sentence into a complex or compound one. Only other clauses do that.

A compound sentence has at least

two independent clauses: *The girl made a fortune on her lemonade stand, and her brother left early to go fishing.* They are independent clauses because each one could stand alone. *The girl made a fortune on her lemonade stand. Her brother left early to go fishing.*

A complex sentence has an independent clause and a subordinate, or dependent, clause. *The girl, who is only five, made a fortune on her lemonade stand.* A subordinate clause *(who is only five)* has a subject and predicate but can't stand alone. *Who is only five* doesn't work as a sentence by itself. Sometimes what could be an independent clause is turned into a subordinate clause by the conjunction you use. Suppose instead of *and* in the compound sentence, we had *because,* so the sentence read: *The girl made a fortune on her lemonade stand because her brother left early to go fishing.* The reader is left hanging if you just say *because her brother left early to go fishing,* so adding the word *because* downgrades the clause from an independent one to a subordinate one.

Okay: So a complex sentence is one that has at least two clauses, and at least one of the clauses is dependent, or sub-ordinate, to the independent clause.

There are three kinds of subordinate clauses: adjective, adverbial, and noun. Each does the job of its name. An adjective clause modifies a noun (*who is only five* tells you more about the noun *girl*). Adverbial clauses modify a verb, adjective, or other adverb (but usually a verb). So *because her brother left early to go fishing* tells why she made so much money: no pesky brother there to drink up the profits. Clauses answering *how, when, where,* or *why* are always adverbial. Noun clauses are whole little clauses that do the job of a noun. Usually they act as direct objects. So *she wondered why he left* is a complex sentence with a noun clause as the direct object. (*She* is the subject, *wondered* is the predicate, and *why he left* is the direct object, telling what she wondered.)

Unfortunately, much oral language, especially of the kid variety, lacks complex sentences. Children, and many adults, tend to speak in a loose, run-on sentence kind of construction. "I was going home, you know, and this huge rainstorm started, and I saw my little neighbor sitting at a lemonade stand. She was getting wet—the poor little thing—and I asked if she wanted a ride. She said sure. I even bought up the rest of her lemonade."

A written account of this adventure would probably go something like this: *When I was going home in the middle of a huge rainstorm, I saw my little neighbor sitting at a lemonade stand. Since she was getting wet, I asked her if she'd like a ride. She said sure, so I even bought up the rest of her lemonade.*

Notice that in the example of oral language there are no adjective or adverbial clauses. There is one noun clause: *if she wanted a ride*, since it's the direct object of *asked*. But in the written version there are three adverbial clauses: *When I was going home, Since she was getting wet*, and *so I even bought up the rest of her lemonade.*

Kids whose work is full of run-on sentences are almost always kids who don't do a lot of reading, and so write oral, rather than written, language. They would write the lemonade story like this: *I was going home, this huge rainstorm started, I saw a neighborhood girl sitting at a lemonade stand. She was getting wet, did she want a ride, I asked. She said sure, I bought the rest of her lemonade.* Notice: no subordinate clauses at all.

I find that when students are at this stage in writing, trying to get them to stop writing run-on sentences is like spitting in the wind. They are writing oral language, and not even subordinating ideas in their minds yet. You need to do everything you can to get them reading. It doesn't matter at all what they read, either. Any written language input will help them to start getting a sense of complex sentence structure. Reading is what you need to work on.

5

Once complex sentences start creeping into your children's writing, compliment them and name the sentence construction for them.

So you're looking for your son to write a sentence like this: *The monster ran into his cave because he was frightened.* When that happens, say, "Great sentence! I really like the adverbial clause at the end of it." You don't have to be obnoxious about this, but touch lightly on it if you can.

Name adjective and noun clauses also. Noun clauses are really common—usually acting as direct objects after such predicates as *said, saw, asked, thought,* etc. *She said, "You're really a jerk"* is a complex sentence with the noun clause *You're really a jerk.* Students don't usually make mistakes with noun clauses, since they are commonly used correctly in oral language as well, but they do make mistakes with adjective clauses. The oral statement *Jenna's my sister. She lives here* becomes the run-on *Jenna's my sister, she lives here.* The more sophisticated, complex structure with an adjective clause would be *Jenna, who is my sister, lives here.* So when your children start using sentences like this, praise them, and name the clause.

6

After your children have begun using complex sentences in their writing, and after you've had a chance to familiarize them with the terminology, explain run-on sentences and sentence fragments when they ask for editing help.

Explain that their run-on sentence is two independent clauses, joined with just a comma, when it needs a semicolon or a conjunction. So *I came home early, it was raining* is a run-on sentence. You can fix it by substituting, for the comma, a semicolon *(I came home early; it was raining)* or a period *(I came home early. It was raining)*. Or you can add a conjunction *(I came home early because it was raining)*.

A sentence fragment is either just a phrase *(behind the barn)* or a dependent clause *(when I left)*. It's a group of words that is not a complete thought.

Note that as your children become better and better writers they may occasionally use sentence fragments for emphasis or to establish tone. That's fine. Good writers can do that. They may also write the occasional run-on sentence with two short clauses. This is also fine, especially if it's part of dialogue. The master of run-on sentences in dialogue is Elmore Leonard, who I think is one of the best stylists of our time.

There's a world of difference between the kind of run-on sentences a semiliterate child writes and the kind that a writer like Leonard uses to establish voice.

7 **After your children are using complex sentences easily and frequently in their writing, start pointing out errors of agreement in your friendly "editing" sessions.**

What is an error of agreement? *Everyone should get their lunch boxes from their locker* is the classic example. *Everyone* is singular (because it has a *one* in it) and so needs singular pronouns following it. So the correct, but culturally clumsy, form is *Everyone should get his lunch box from his locker.* The more sensitive, but grammatically clumsy, form is *Everyone should get his or her lunch box from his or her locker.* Neither of these sentences work very well.

No, what you need to tell your children is to avoid using *everyone* or *no one* altogether in sentences that contain other pronouns. Instead, make everything plural. *All students should get their lunch boxes from their lockers.* Even better, drop the stuffy tone and say, *Hey, kids, get your lunch boxes from your lockers.*

Your children also need to watch for sentences that start with singular asexual nouns like *teenager* or *driver* because you end up with sentences like this: *If your teenager comes in late, explain to him (or her?) that you were worried.* Again, the only solution is to make the whole thing plural, or completely rewrite.

The field of grammar has become, finally, a little bit interesting these days because of pronoun agreement wars. The purists want to maintain the masculine form as a sort of neutral singular pronoun. *Everyone should get his lunch box* is just fine with them. Politically correct, but tone-deaf, writers drop *his or her* phrases all over the place. Some writers randomly use *his* in some places and *her* in others. And some are just closing their eyes and using the incorrect form *(Everyone should get their lunch boxes)* because it has so overwhelmed the grammatically correct form in everyday speech that it sounds right to most people.

But, personally, I think the incorrect form sounds tacky, and marks the user of it as a less than classy writer. So teach your kids to spot pronoun agreement problems and then write around them.

8

After your children understand pronoun agreement, start paying attention to parallel construction in their writing.

Do this by first noticing when your kids use parallel construction correctly. If your daughter writes *I like dancing and singing,* say, "I like how you use those two gerunds"—verbal nouns, remember?—"for your two direct objects. It's much better than if you had written *I like singing and to dance* because then you would have used one gerund [singing] and one infinitive [to dance] and it wouldn't have balanced."

Notice that being able to recognize gerunds and infinitives becomes important in parallel construction discussions, so if you hadn't been using the terms, start using them now.

The most common error is when kids try to balance a phrase with a clause. *I like coming late to class because it's fun, and to get my teacher angry.* I tell them to rewrite it using the same kind of construction all the way through. This, for example, would work better: *I like coming late to class because it's fun, and because my teacher gets angry.* Even better would be a complete rewrite: *Coming to class late is fun and gets my teacher angry.* And even better than that, tell them, would be coming to class on time.

9 **After you've come this far with grammar, start asking your children occasionally to look over your writing and make editing suggestions.**

After your kids have the fundamentals of grammar down, it helps them to look at writing other than their own with a critical eye. If you've done your job well, you'll probably see that they pick up errors or awkwardnesses in your writing that you've completely overlooked. And that's great, right?

While they're editing your work, you can model for them the proper behavior of the editee, so to speak. Listen carefully to their suggestions, seriously consider their worth, and then follow the suggestions that make sense to you. Tell them that authors should always have the final say over their work.

10

Keep a grammar book nearby for usage issues that come up.

The final grammar stage is being able and willing to use a grammar book. The best place to find one is in college bookstores, so arrange a grammar book–buying trip with your kids. See if you can find several to look through and compare. Personally, I like short, concise grammar guides, such as *Elements of Style,* by William Strunk and E. B. White, or *A Pocket Style Manual,* by Diana Hacker.

Now you can start getting in little grammar discussions. Does punctuation *always* go inside quotation marks? What about if the marks are around only one word? What's a dangling participle? Should you use *affect* or *effect* in a particular sentence? (They'll find out that *affect* is a verb and *effect* is a noun. See how important those parts of speech are.)

When you're at this point with your children, you're home-free, grammar wise. Now you just have to watch that they don't become that most dreaded of bores, the Perfect Grammar Person who corrects everyone else.

Definitely discourage that.

About the Author

Mary Leonhardt, the author of *Parents Who Love Reading, Kids Who Don't*, *Keeping Kids Reading*, and *99 Ways to Get Kids to Love Reading*, has taught English in public, private, and parochial schools for twenty-eight years. She is currently at Concord-Carlisle High School in Massachusetts.